Animal Offspring

Gorillas and Their Infants

Revised Edition

Margaret Hall

Raintree is an imprint of Capstone Global Library Limited, a company incorporated in England and Wales having its registered office at 264 Banbury Road, Oxford, OX2 7DY – Registered company number: 6695582

www.raintree.co.uk
myorders@raintree.co.uk

ISBN 978 1 4747 5628 0 (hardback)
22 21 20 19 18
10 9 8 7 6 5 4 3 2 1

ISBN 978 1 4747 5638 9 (paperback)
23 22 21 20 19
10 9 8 7 6 5 4 3 2 1

British Library Cataloging in Publication Data
A full catalogue record for this book is available from the British Library.

Editorial Credits
Gina Kammer, editor; Sarah Bennett, designer;
Morgan Walters, media researcher; Katy LaVigne, production specialist

Printed and bound in India.

Acknowledgements
We would like to thank the following for permission to reproduce photographs:
Shutterstock: abxyz, right 20, blojfo, 19, Edwin Butter, left 20, left 21, Fiona Ayerst, 7, GUDKOV ANDREY, Cover, islavicek, 13, Kiki Dohmeier, 17, LMspencer, 15, meunierd, right 21, Nick Fox, 11, Simon Eeman, 1, 5, Stayer, 9

Every effort has been made to contact copyright holders of material reproduced in this book. Any omissions will be rectified in subsequent printings if notice is given to the publisher.

All the Internet addresses (URLs) given in this book were valid at the time of going to press. However, due to the dynamic nature of the Internet, some addresses may have changed, or sites may have changed or ceased to exist since publication. While the author and publisher regret any inconvenience this may cause readers, no responsibility for any such changes can be accepted by either the author or the publisher.

Contents

Gorillas

Gorillas are strong mammals. Young gorillas are called infants. Gorillas and their infants live in Africa.

Gorillas live in family groups called troops. A male gorilla is a silverback. A silverback mates with a female gorilla.

The infant

A female gorilla usually gives birth to one infant.

Infants drink milk

from their mothers.

Infants sometimes ride on
the backs of their mothers.

Growing up

Infants grow and become young gorillas. Young gorillas play and climb.

Young gorillas learn
to find food.
Gorillas eat plants
and bark.

Young gorillas leave
the troop after about
eight years. Then they
live with a new troop.

Watch gorillas grow

birth

adult after
about ten years

21

Glossary

Africa one of the seven continents of the world

infant very young animal; a gorilla infant depends on its mother for 3 to 5 years

mammal warm-blooded animal that has a backbone; mammals have hair or fur and feed milk to their young; gorillas have thick hair

mate join together to produce young

silverback adult male gorilla; silverbacks have grey or silver hair on their backs

troop group of animals that lives or moves together; a troop works together to teach young gorillas how to live and find food

Find out more

Books

Gorilla (Animals on the Edge), Anna Claybourne (Bloomsbury Childrens, 2012)

Jungle Animals (Animals in Their Habitats), Sian Smith (Raintree, 2015)

The Life Cycle of Mammals (Life Cycles), Susan H. Gray (Raintree, 2012)

Websites

www.awf.org/wildlife-conservation/mountain-gorilla
African Wildlife Foundation

www.dkfindout.com/us/animals-and-nature/primates/gorillas/
DK Find Out!

Comprehension questions

1. What kinds of things do young gorillas do?

2. Where in this book can you find out why male gorillas are called silverbacks?

3. How does a mother gorilla care for her infant?

Index